BIG ENGLISH 1

GW00599272

Contents

Welcome to Class!

1 **Look, read and match.**

1

a
> Hello, I'm Patrick.

2

b
> Hello, I'm Jane.

3

c
> Hello, I'm Maria.

2 **Draw and write.**

> What's your name?

> Hello, I'm _____.

3 **Look and circle.**

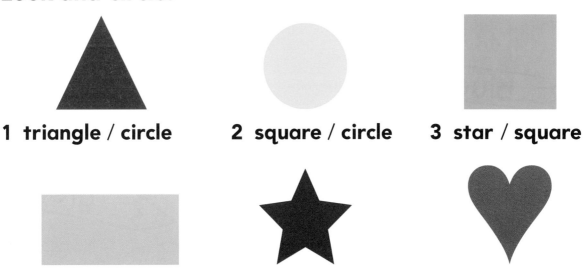

1 triangle / circle   **2 square / circle**   **3 star / square**

4 rectangle / triangle   **5 star / rectangle**   **6 star / heart**

4 **Read and draw.**

1 It's a triangle.   **2** It's a star.   **3** It's a heart.

5 **Read and colour.**

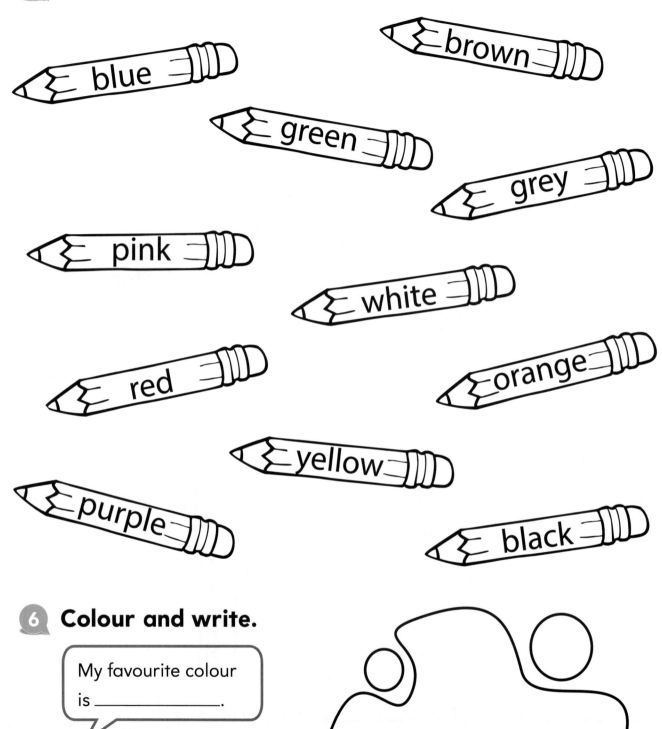

blue

brown

green

grey

pink

white

red

orange

yellow

purple

black

6 **Colour and write.**

My favourite colour
is _____.

7 **Read and match.**

one

two

three

four

five

six

seven

eight

nine

ten

eleven

twelve

thirteen

fourteen

fifteen

8 **Join the dots. Write.**

It's a _____ .

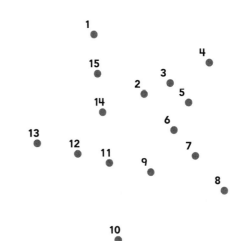

9 **Draw and write. How old are you?**

I'm _____ .

Good Morning, Class!

1 **Match, colour and say.**

1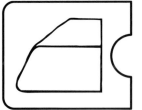

a  book

2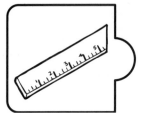

b 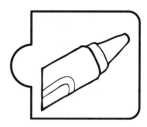 crayon

3

c 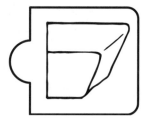 rubber

4

d 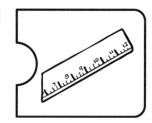 ruler

2 **Look and circle.**

1 What is it?

It's a **pen / marker pen**.

2 What is it?

It's a **backpack / desk**.

3 Listen and sing. Then draw.

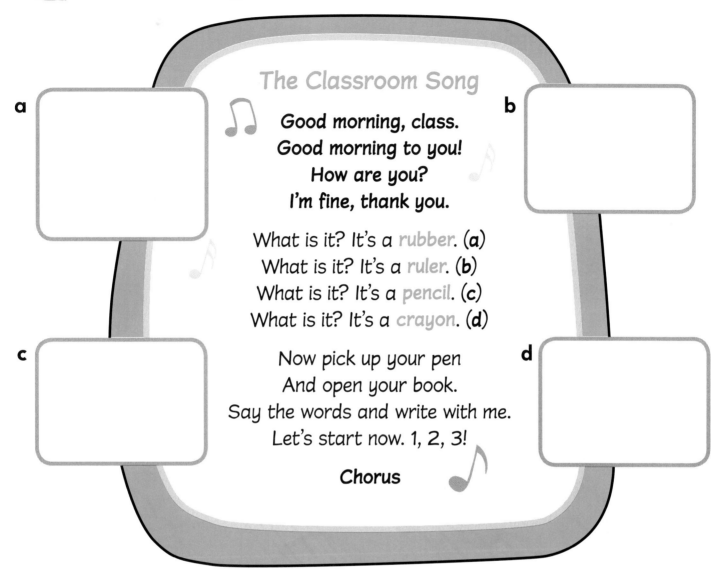

a

b

The Classroom Song

Good morning, class.
Good morning to you!
How are you?
I'm fine, thank you.

What is it? It's a rubber. (**a**)
What is it? It's a ruler. (**b**)
What is it? It's a pencil. (**c**)
What is it? It's a crayon. (**d**)

Now pick up your pen
And open your book.
Say the words and write with me.
Let's start now. 1, 2, 3!

Chorus

c

d

4 Draw your backpack. Then write.

This is my _____.

It's _____.

5 **Read and circle.**

6 **Listen and colour.** 1:25

1  2  3  4

Complete the sequence.

THINK BIG

1 2 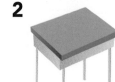 3 4

1:27
7 Listen and ✓.

1 a  ☐   b  ☐

2 a  ☐   b  ☐

3 a 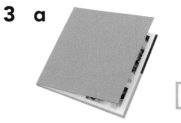 ☐   b  ☐

4 a  ☐   b  ☐

8 Read, draw and colour.

1 It's a pencil.
It's green.

2 It's a book.
It's blue.

3 It's a crayon.
It's yellow.

What are they?

They're...

9 Match and say.

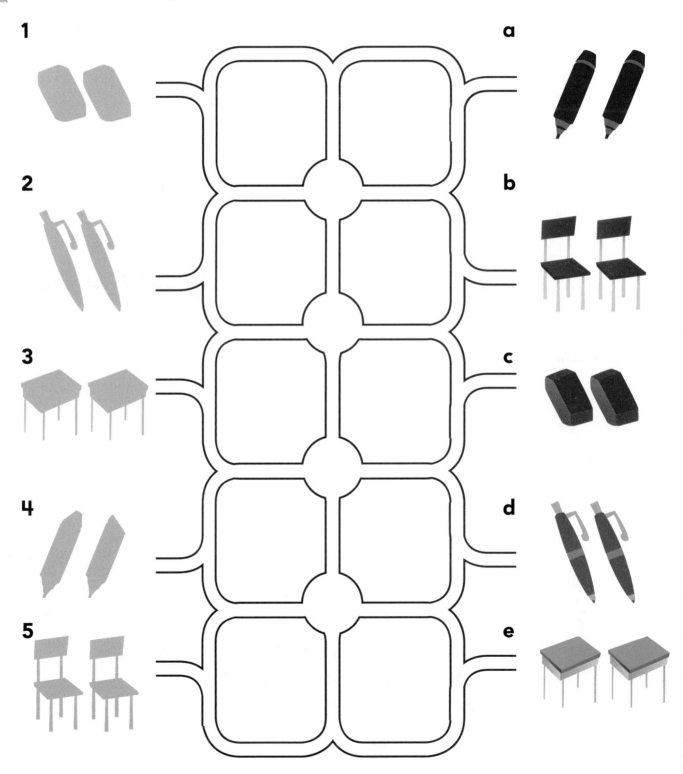

10 **Look and circle.**

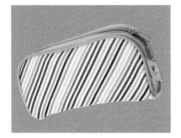

1 It's a **pencil case / pencil sharpener**.

2 It's a **notebook / tablet**.

3 It's a **pencil / pencil sharpener**.

4 It's a **tablet / notebook**.

11 **Count and write.**

1  **2** **3** **4**

_____ rubbers   _____ marker pens   _____ rulers   _____ desk

THINK BIG

I've got 3 green pens and 1 red pen. How many pens have I got?
I've got _____ pens.

12 **Read and write.**

> Please   welcome   you

1

Thank you.

You're _____.

2

_____ sit down.

Thank _____.

13 **Draw.**

I'm polite at school.

14 **Find and circle the letters a, t, p and n.**

15 **Read and circle the letters a, t, p and n.**

1 and   **2** ten   **3** pen   **4** nip

16 **Match the words with the same sounds.**

1 nap   **a** pen
2 pan   **b** and
3 ant   **c** nip

1:37
17 **Listen and chant.**

Pat the ant

Has got a tan.

Pat the ant

Takes a nap.

18 **Read, draw and colour.**

1 I've got a pencil. It's yellow.

2 I've got a desk. It's blue.

3 I've got three marker pens.
They're red.

4 I've got two books.
They're green.

19 **Read and circle.**

1 What is it?
It's / They're a tablet.

2 What are they?
It's / They're notebooks.

3 What is it? It's a
pencil case / pencil sharpener.

4 What **is it / are they**?
They're pencil sharpeners.

20 **Draw.**

My desk and
my chair:

21 Colour.

1 = **red**   2 = blue   3 = **green**   4 = yellow

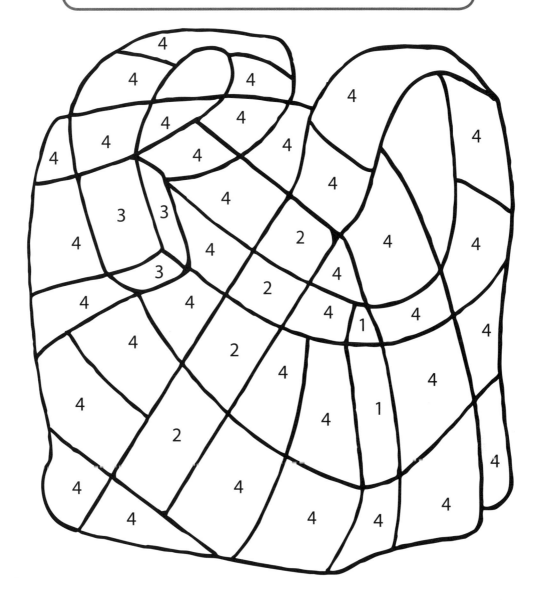

22 Look at 21. Match.

1 What is it? It's red.

2 What is it? It's blue.

3 What is it? It's green.

4 What is it? It's yellow.

a It's a rubber.

b It's a backpack.

c It's a crayon.

d It's a ruler.

unit 2

My Family

1 **Read and match.**

grandma

grandad

sister

My family.

brother

dad

mum

2 Listen and circle. Then sing.

My Family

My family, my family!
This is my family.
He's my brother / sister
And she's my brother / sister.

My dad / mum, my dad / mum!
My sister, my brother!
We have so much fun!
I love them!

My family, my family.
I love my family!
I love them and they love me.
I love my family!

3 Draw your mum and dad. Then write.

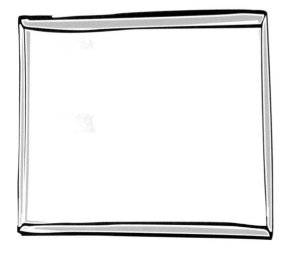

My _____

My _____

4 **Read and point. Then read and circle.**

A Big Family

Who are they?

They're my parents.

Who's she?

She's my sister.

Oh, she's Jane.

And who's he?

He's my brother!

How many brothers and sisters have I got?

I've got...

a one brother and two sisters.

b one brother and one sister.

c two brothers and one sister.

THINK BIG

Tick (✓) Tim's family.

1 ☐ 2 ☐

1:48

5 **Listen and write the number.**

6 Read. Count and colour.

7 **Look, read and match.**

1    2    3    4

a boy   **b** man   **c** woman   **d** girl

8 **Look at the picture. Then read and circle.**

This is my family.

1 I'm a **boy** / **girl**.

2 This **man** / **woman** is my dad.

3 This **boy** / **baby** is my brother.

4 This **girl** / **boy** is my sister.

5 This **girl** / **woman** is my mum.

THINK BIG

Are you a boy or a girl?

I'm a _____.

9 **Listen and match.**

1

a Tommy helps his mum. **b** Pam helps her brother.

2

10 **Draw.**

I can help!

11 **Find and circle the letters i, s, b and d.**

12 **Read and circle the letters i, s, b and d.**

1 dad   **2** in   **3** bat   **4** sit

13 **Match the words with the same sounds.**

1 dad   **a** sad
2 in   **b** dip
3 sit   **c** it

14 **Listen and chant.**

1:59

Don't sit, sit, sit
On a pin, pin, pin
It's bad, bad, bad
To sit on a pin!

15 **Find the family words. Colour them green.**

My Family

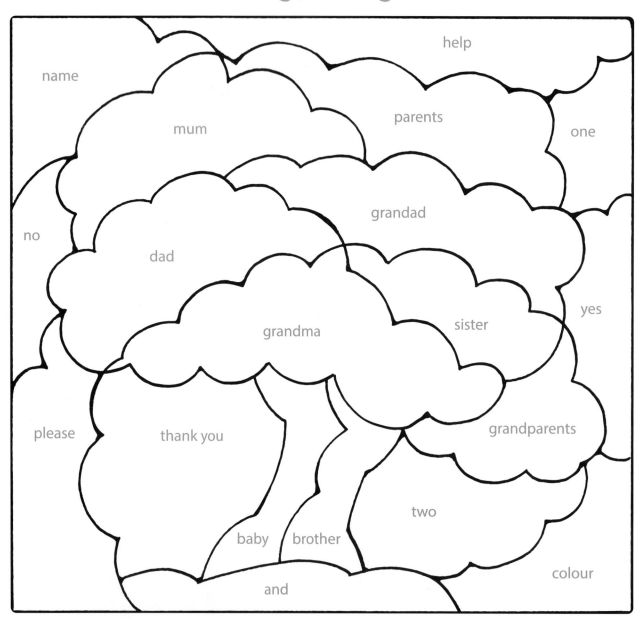

help

name

mum

parents

one

grandad

no

dad

grandma

sister

yes

please

thank you

grandparents

two

baby

brother

colour

and

16 **Circle. Who's in your family?**

I've got   a mum   a dad   a sister   a brother

a grandma   a grandad

17 **Look and match. Then read.**

1   **a** man

2   **b** girl

3   **c** boy

4   **d** woman

18 **Draw your family. Then say.**

This is my family.

My Body

1 **Read and match.**

eye   head

nose   ear

neck   mouth

leg   finger

hand   arm

toe   foot

2 **Draw your friend.**

3 **Listen and circle. Then sing.**

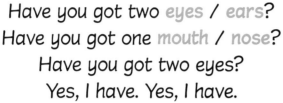

My Body Song

Have you got two eyes / ears?
Have you got one mouth / nose?
Have you got two eyes?
Yes, I have. Yes, I have.

I've got ten fingers / toes.
I've got ten toes.
I've got two hands / feet
And one big nose!

And have you got long hair / legs?
And have you got short hair / arms?
And have you got small hands?
I sing my body song, my body song,
I sing my body song again!

4 **Read and write.**

| one | ten | ten | two | two |

1 I've got _____ fingers.

2 I've got _____ nose.

3 I've got _____ toes.

4 I've got _____ ears.

5 I've got _____ eyes.

5 **Read and match.**

a Yes, he has! Bobo has got one eye!

b No. My teddy bear has got small ears.

Lost Teddy

Is this your teddy bear?

_____

Brown? Oh! Has he got one eye?

_____

6 **Read and circle Yes or No.**

1 Is Bobo green? **Yes** **No**

2 Has Bobo got small ears? **Yes** **No**

3 Has he got long legs? **Yes** **No**

4 Has he got one eye? **Yes** **No**

THINK BIG

This is _____. He's my favourite teddy bear.
He's got **big / small** eyes.
He's got **big / small** ears.
He's got **short / long** legs.

7 **Read, match and circle.**

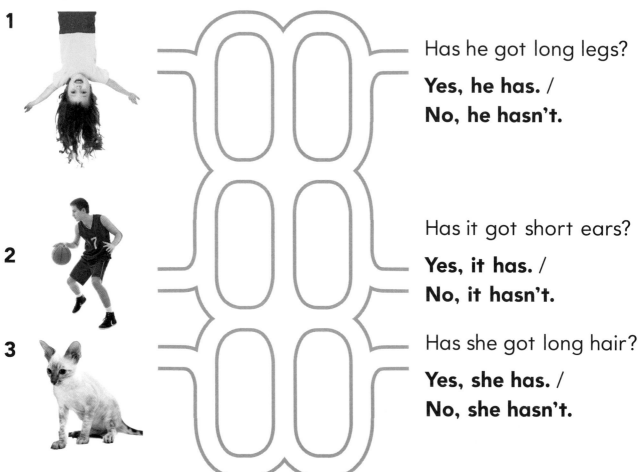

1

Has he got long legs?

**Yes, he has. /
No, he hasn't.**

2

Has it got short ears?

**Yes, it has. /
No, it hasn't.**

3

Has she got long hair?

**Yes, she has. /
No, she hasn't.**

1:70

8 **Listen and ✓.**

1   a   b

2   a   b

9 **Join numbers 1 to 10. What is it?**

10 **Look at 9. Circle the answer.**

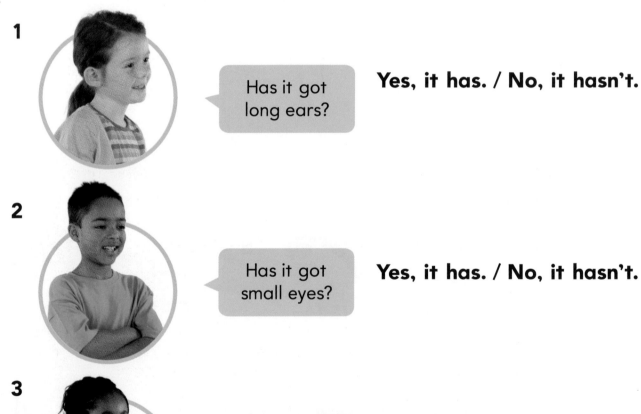

1 Has it got long ears? **Yes, it has. / No, it hasn't.**

2 Has it got small eyes? **Yes, it has. / No, it hasn't.**

3 Has it got a big nose? **Yes, it has. / No, it hasn't.**

11 Look and circle. Then match.

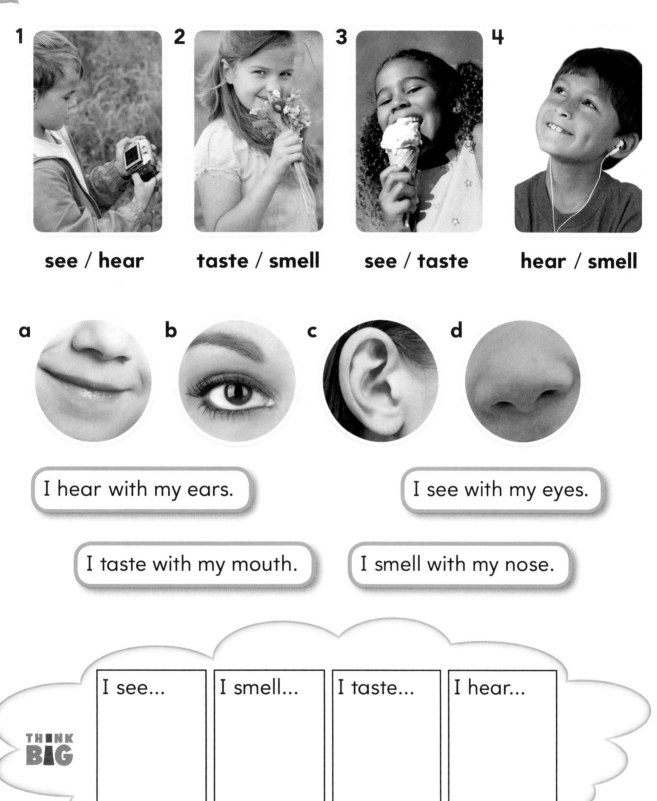

1 see / hear

2 taste / smell

3 see / taste

4 hear / smell

a

b

c

d

I hear with my ears.

I see with my eyes.

I taste with my mouth.

I smell with my nose.

THINK BIG

I see...

I smell...

I taste...

I hear...

1:77

12 Listen and match. Then sing.

Keep Clean ♪

1
Every day
Before I eat
And after I play
I wash my hands.

a

2
With a lot of soap
It's easy, you see.
Rinse with water
Just like me.

b

3
Dry them well and
Sing this song.
Keep your hands clean
All day long!

c

13 Draw.

I keep
clean.

14 **Find and circle the letters e, c, g and m.**

15 **Read and circle the letters e, c, g and m.**

1 gas **2** map **3** cap **4** pen

16 **Match the words with the same sounds.**

1 get   **a** cat
2 mat   **b** map
3 cap   **c** gas

1:82
17 **Listen and chant.**

The cap is on the cat.

The cat goes on the map.

The pen goes on the bed.

18 **Read and circle.**

1

Has he got a long nose?

Yes, he has. / No, he hasn't.

2

Has he got small feet?

Yes, he has. / No, he hasn't.

3

Has he got short hair?

Yes, he has. / No, he hasn't.

19 **Look at 18. Read and circle.**

1 Has Meg got short hair?

Yes, she has. / No, she hasn't.

2 Has Meg got big eyes?

Yes, she has. / No, she hasn't.

20 Look and write.

arm

eye

finger

leg

mouth

nose

1 _____

3 _____

5 _____

2 _____

4 _____

6 _____

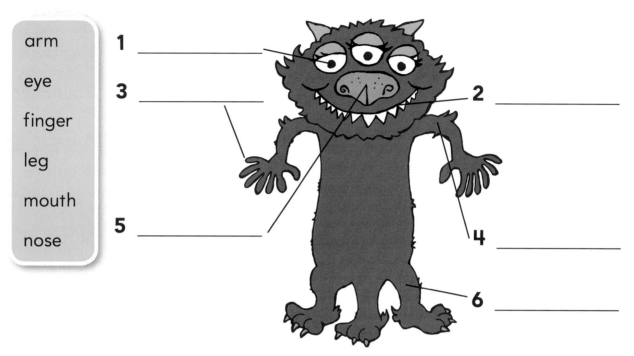

21 Draw and match.

This is me.

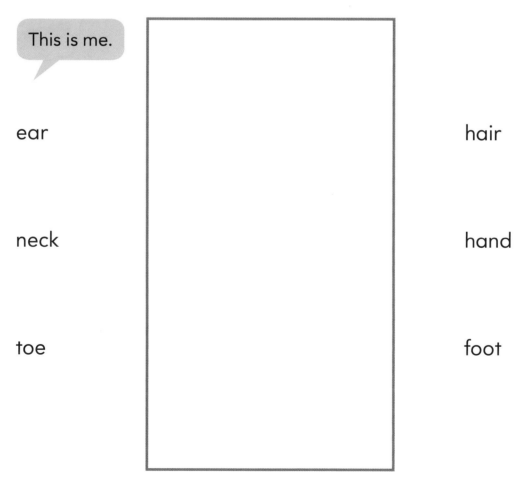

ear   hair

neck   hand

toe   foot

1 Look, find and number.

CLASS

1	crayons
2	rubbers
3	pens
4	rulers

2 Look and ✓.
Tom's got:

My List

☐ pens

☐ pencils

☐ rubbers

☐ a ruler

3 Think and draw. Tom hasn't got:

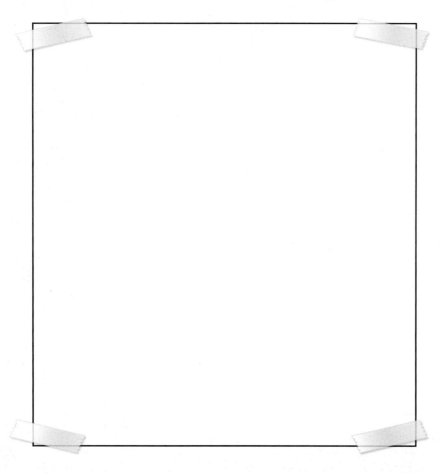

FAMILY

5 dad

6 mum

7 sister

BODY

8 arm

9 eye

10 hand

My Favourite Clothes

1 **Colour. Then match.**

| a red blouse | blue trousers | a yellow jacket |

1 = **red**

2 = **blue**

3 = yellow

| yellow boots | a blue skirt | red shoes | red gloves |

2 **Draw.**

My Favourite Clothes

3 Listen and circle. Then chant.

What Are You Wearing?

What are you wearing?
I'm wearing a T-shirt / shirt.
What are you wearing?
I'm wearing a skirt / blouse.

What's he wearing?
He's wearing new trousers / shorts.
What's he wearing?
He's wearing old shoes / boots.

What's she wearing?
She's wearing a red / blue hat.
What's she wearing?
She's wearing black / pink shoes.

4 **Match. Then read and colour.**

Which clothes are the same? Circle.

THINK BIG

2:09

5 **Listen and ✓.**

1 a ☐ b ☐ 2 a ☐ b ☐

3 a ☐ b ☐ 4 a ☐ b ☐

6 **Look. Read and circle.**

I'm wearing **boots / shoes**, a hat and a **green / yellow** jacket.

I'm wearing a **green / yellow** T-shirt, trousers and blue **boots / shoes**.

1   2

7 **Colour and write.**

b = **brown**	g = **green**	o = orange
p = **purple**	r = **red**	y = yellow

1 He's wearing an orange _____.

2 He's wearing a yellow _____.

3 He's wearing purple _____.

4 He's wearing brown _____.

5 He's wearing green _____.

gloves

shoes

shirt

hat

trousers

8 Find, write and circle.

desert   jungle   mountains

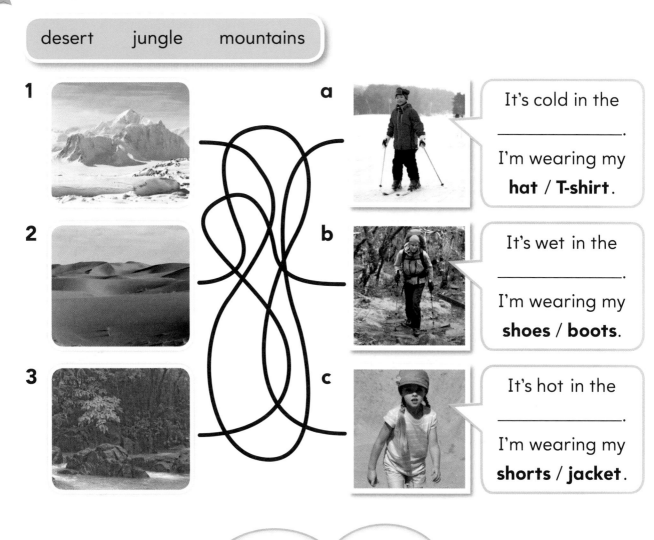

1 a

It's cold in the
_____.
I'm wearing my
hat / T-shirt.

2 b

It's wet in the
_____.
I'm wearing my
shoes / boots.

3 c

It's hot in the
_____.
I'm wearing my
shorts / jacket.

It's wet. What's she wearing? Circle.

THINK BIG

jacket   trousers
dress   blouse
shorts   shirt
boots   shoes
hat   skirt
socks
gloves

9 Look, read and write.

dress   trousers   white

They're wearing traditional clothes from the Philippines. He's wearing a _____ shirt and _____. She's wearing a white _____.

10 Draw.

I'm wearing traditional clothes.

11 **Find and circle the letters o, k and ck.**

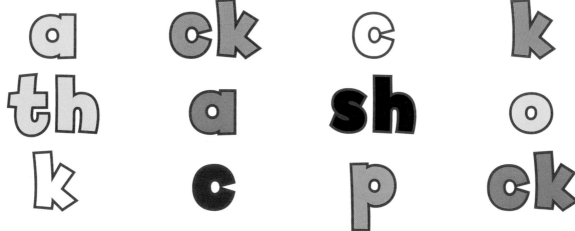

12 **Read and circle the letters o, k and ck.**

1 on   **2** kid   **3** sock   **4** dog

13 **Match the words with the same sounds.**

1 pot   **a** pick
2 neck   **b** kit
3 kid   **c** dog

2:18
14 **Listen and chant.**

Put on your socks,
Put on your kit.
Kick the ball,
Kick, kick, kick!

15 **Look and write.**

| blouse | boots | dress | gloves | hat | jacket | shirt |
| shoes | shorts | skirt | socks | trousers | T-shirt |

1 _____

2 _____

3 _____

4 _____

5 _____

6 _____

7 _____

8 _____

9 _____

10 _____

11 _____

12 _____

13 _____

2:20

16 Look and colour. Then listen and ✓.

1 = **green**	2 = yellow	3 = **black**
4 = blue	5 = orange	6 = **purple**

17 What are you wearing? Write.

a blouse   a jacket   a shirt   a skirt
boots   trousers   shoes

I'm wearing _____ .

unit 5

Busy at Home

1 **Read and match.**

1 She's getting dressed. ☐

2 She's drinking and he's reading. ☐

3 He's having a bath. ☐

4 He's making lunch. ☐

5 He's eating. ☐

2 Listen and write. Then sing.

breakfast   face   hair   lunch   phone   teeth

What Are You Doing?

I'm brushing my ¹_____.
I'm combing my ²_____.
I'm busy. I'm busy.
What are you doing?

I'm eating my ³_____.
I'm washing my ⁴_____.
I'm busy. I'm busy.
What are you doing?

I'm talking on the ⁵_____.
I'm making my ⁶_____.
I'm busy. I'm busy.
What are you doing?

Chorus

3 Draw.

He's sleeping.	She's playing.

4 **Read and write.**

Fun at Home

What are you doing, boys?

We're playing.

It's time for lunch! What are you doing now?

I'm drawing.

I'm drawing, too.

1 What are they doing?

They're _____.

2 What is Patrick doing?

He's _____.

Boys, I'm making lunch.

3 What's she doing?

She's _____.

THINK BIG

What are you and your friend doing?

We're _____.

5 **Listen and number.**

a

b

c

d

e

6 **Circle.**

1  **He's / She's** sleeping.

2  **He's / She's** talking on the phone.

3  **He's / She's** drinking.

7 **Write I'm, He's or She's.**

1 What's she doing? _____ washing.

2 What are you doing? _____ having a bath.

3 What's he doing? _____ combing his hair.

8 **Look and match.**

1 What are you doing, Dad?   **a** I'm drawing.

2 What are you doing, Anna?   **b** I'm reading.

3 What are you doing, Mum?   **c** I'm eating.

4 What are you doing, Grandad?   **d** I'm making lunch.

9 **Draw. What are you doing?**

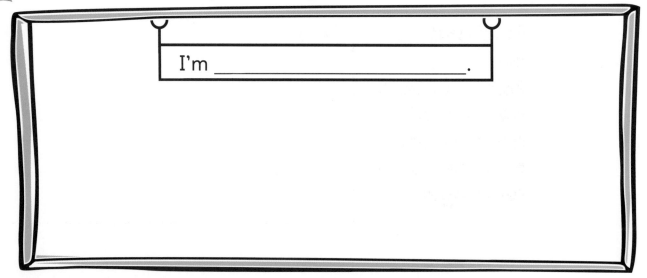

I'm _____.

10 **Read and write.**

| houseboat | flat | lighthouse | yurt |

1 _____ 2 _____ 3 _____ 4 _____

11 **Look, read and circle.**

 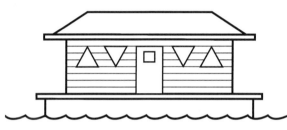

1 It's a **lighthouse** / **flat**.
It's got **six** / **seven** windows.
They're **circles** / **squares**.

2 It's a **yurt** / **houseboat**.
It's got **four** / **five** windows.
They're **triangles** / **circles**.

THINK BIG

Find and draw three things in your house that are a square, a circle and a rectangle.

2:36

12 Listen and write.

| cleaning | drying | helping | washing |

1 She's _____ her room.

2 She's _____ the dishes.

3 He's _____ the dishes.

4 She's _____ her parents.

13 Draw.

I'm helping at home.

14 **Find and circle the letters u, f and ff.**

15 **Read and circle the letters u, f and ff.**

1 up   **2** fan   **3** puff   **4** bus

16 **Match the words with the same sounds.**

1 sun   **a** fan
2 off   **b** up
3 fog   **c** puff

2:41
17 **Listen and chant.**

We're having fun,
Running in the sun.
Up, up, up!
Puff, puff, puff!

18 Look and match.

a

b

c

d

e

f

g

h

i

j

k

l

1 I'm brushing my teeth.

2 I'm having a bath.

3 I'm making lunch.

4 I'm eating.

5 I'm sleeping.

6 I'm playing.

7 I'm combing my hair.

8 I'm drinking.

9 I'm reading.

10 I'm talking on the phone.

11 I'm washing my face.

12 I'm getting dressed.

19 **Look and write.**

eating   having   reading

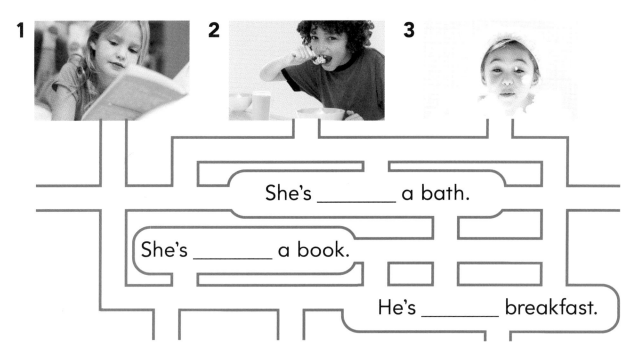

1

2

3

She's _____ a bath.

She's _____ a book.

He's _____ breakfast.

20 **Colour shapes. What is it?**

☐ = **green**

○ = **black**

▭ = **yellow**

△ = **red**

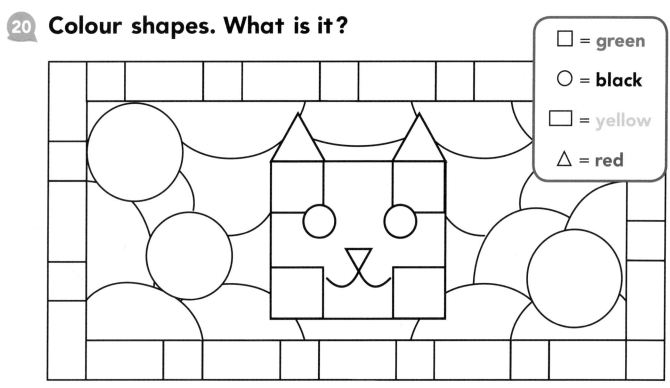

What is it?   It's a c__t.

On the Farm

1 **Look and write. Then circle.**

cow   duck   horse

1

It's a ___COW___.
It's (eating) / flying.

2

It's a ___horse___.
It's sleeping / (running).

3

It's a ___duck___.
It's running / (flying).

2 Listen and match. Then chant.

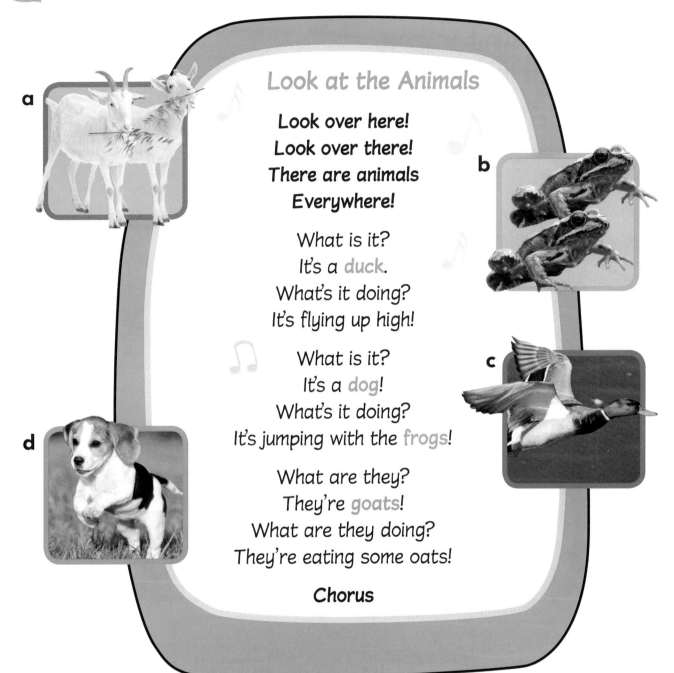

Look at the Animals

Look over here!
Look over there!
There are animals
Everywhere!

What is it?
It's a duck.
What's it doing?
It's flying up high!

What is it?
It's a dog!
What's it doing?
It's jumping with the frogs!

What are they?
They're goats!
What are they doing?
They're eating some oats!

Chorus

a

b

c

d

3 Write. Then draw.

This is my favourite
farm animal. Look.
It's a _____.

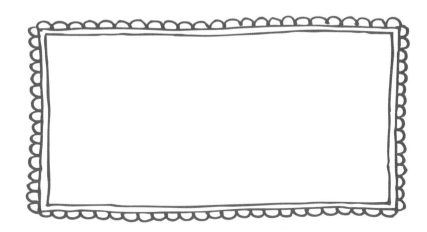

4 Read and number.

Oh, no! It's eating your skirt! ☐

It's jumping. ☐

They're running. ☐

It's flying. ☐

Which sentence is wrong? Tick (✓) or cross (✗).

The frog is jumping. ☐   The cat is flying. ☐

The horse is running. ☐

2:52

5 Listen and number.

6 Look and write.

eating   flying   jumping   running

1 It's _____.

2 It's _____.

3 It's _____.

4 It's _____.

7 **Look and circle.**

1 It's / They're jumping.

2 It's / They're eating.

3 It's / They're flying.

4 It's / They're running.

8 **Draw.**

What's the cat doing?
It's sleeping.

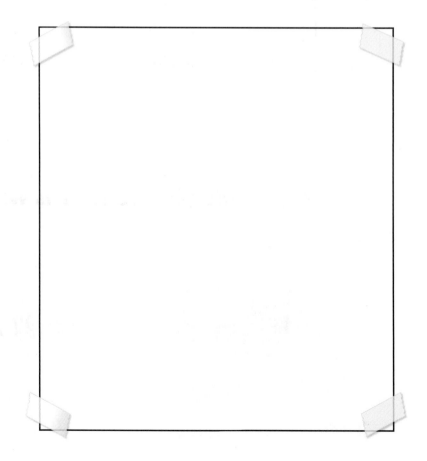

9 ## Colour, match and circle.

1 This cow is black and white.

2 This chicken is red.

3 This dog is brown.

4 This cat is black.

a

b

c

d

A baby chicken is a **calf** / **chick**.

A baby dog is a **kitten** / **puppy**.

A baby cat is a **calf** / **kitten**.

A baby cow is a **puppy** / **calf**.

Circle the picture that is wrong.

THINK BIG

a

b

c

2:58

10 Listen and write. Then match.

brushing   feeding   playing   walking

a  ☐

b  ☐

c  ☐

d  ☐

1 I'm _____ the dog.

2 I'm _____ with the cat.

3 I'm _____ the chicks.

4 I'm _____ the horse.

11 Draw.

I'm playing with the cat.

12 **Find and circle the letters r, h and j.**

13 **Read and circle the letters r, h and j.**

1 [rat]   **2** [hat]   **3** [jam]   **4** [run]

14 **Match the words with the same sounds.**

1 red   **a** hut
2 hen   **b** rock
3 jam   **c** job

2:63

15 **Listen and chant.**

A red hen in
A red hat
Is eating red jam.
Run, red hen, run!

16 **Look, read and circle.**

1

1 It's a **dog** / **cat**.

2 It's a **goat** / **dog**.

2

3 It's a **cow** / **sheep**.

4 It's a **frog** / **sheep**.

4

5 It's a **turtle** / **horse**.

3

6 It's a **chicken** / **horse**.

6

5

7 It's a **duck** / **chicken**.

8 It's a **frog** / **dog**.

8

7

9 It's a **cat** / **chicken**.

10 It's a **goat** / **cow**.

9

10

17 **Look and read. Then circle and write.**

eating   flying   jumping   running   sleeping

What are they doing?

1 What are they doing?
It's / They're

_____.

2 What's it doing?
It's / They're

_____.

3 What are they doing?
It's / They're

_____.

4 What's it doing?
It's / They're

_____.

5 What are they doing?
It's / They're

_____.

18 **Choose and draw.**

calf
chick
kitten
puppy

This is a baby animal.

It's a _____.

THINK BIG

1 **Look, find and number.**

2 **Look and ✓.**
What is Sue wearing?

- [ ] a hat
- [ ] a T-shirt
- [ ] boots
- [ ] trousers
- [ ] a jacket

CLOTHES

1 dress
2 shoes
3 trousers
4 shirt

Look at 1 and draw.
What other animals can you see?

AT HOME

5 sleeping
6 talking on the phone
7 drinking

ANIMALS

8 cat
9 duck
10 turtle

Party Time

1 Match.

1

2

milk | fruit
a | b
c | d
juice | pizza

3

4

2 Look at 1. Write.

1 She's drinking <u>juice</u>. **2** He's drinking <u>milk</u>.

3 He's eating <u>pizza</u>. **4** She's eating <u>fruit</u>.

Listen and number. Then sing.

a

b

It's My Party!

Welcome, friends.
Please sit down.
It's time for my party!
With games and a clown!

I've got pizza, chicken, (**1**)
Salad, too. (**2**)
Fruit, cake (**3**)
And ice cream for you! (**4**)

Or put some pasta (**5**)
On your plate.
With juice or milk (**6**)
It sure tastes great.

Thanks for the presents.
What a great day!
Let's eat and drink
And play, play, play.

c

d

f

e

4 **Draw.**

I'm eating chips and I'm drinking water.

5 **Read and write.**

1 Tim's party is on _____.

2 Tim's got _____.

3 Maria's got _____.

4 Patrick's got _____ and _____.

THINK BIG

Write the days in order.
Then circle your favourite day.

Monday _____ _____ Thursday

_____ Saturday _____

6 **Look and write.**

I've got fruit.   I've got pizza.

What have you got?

1 _____

2 _____

7 **Read and draw.**

1 I've got chicken.

2 I've got ice cream.

8 **Draw. Then write.**

cake   fruit   ice cream   juice   pizza

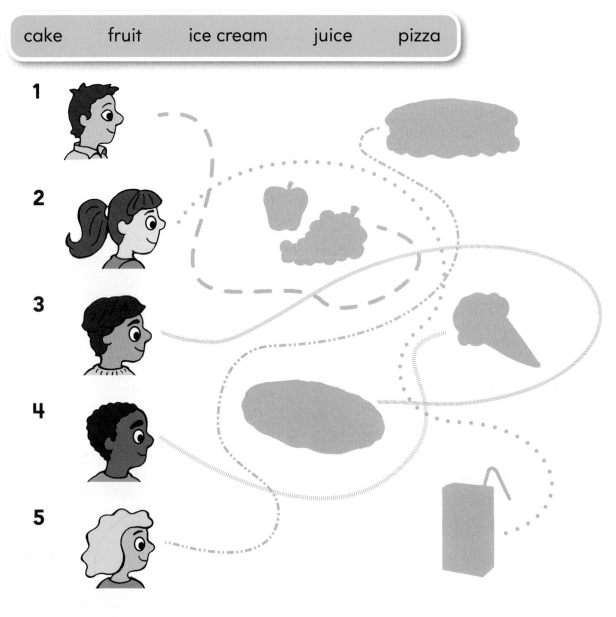

1 What's he got?   He's got _____.

2 What's she got?   She's got _____.

3 What's he got?   He's _____.

4 What's he got?   _____

5 What's she got?   _____

3:13

9 **Listen and number. Then write.**

| biscuits | chips | chocolate | crisps | salt | sugar |

a
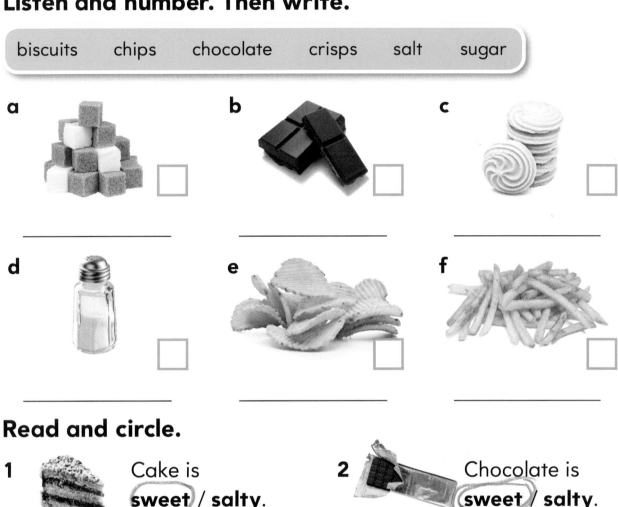

_____

b

_____

c

_____

d

_____

e

_____

f

_____

10 **Read and circle.**

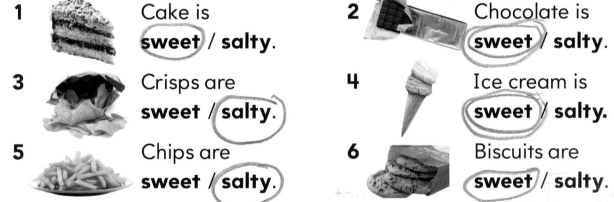

1 Cake is
(sweet) / salty.

2 Chocolate is
(sweet) / salty.

3 Crisps are
sweet / (salty).

4 Ice cream is
(sweet) / salty.

5 Chips are
sweet / (salty).

6 Biscuits are
(sweet) / salty.

Draw and write.

THINK
BIG

_____ sweet.

_____ salty.

11 **Look and write.**

breakfast   dinner   lunch

1 I eat _____ every day.

2 I eat _____ every day.

3 I eat _____ every day.

12 **Draw.**

This is my dinner. I'm eating _____ and _____. I'm drinking _____.

13 **Find and circle the letters l, ll, v and w.**

14 **Read and circle the letters l, ll, v and w.**

1 van   **2** leg   **3** web   **4** doll

15 **Match the words with the same sounds.**

1 let	**a** sell
2 bell	**b** leg
3 vet	**c** win
4 we	**d** van

3:19
16 **Listen and chant.**

Let's ring the bell
For the vet
With the van!

3:21

17 **Listen and match. Then write.**

1 I've got _water_.

2 I've got _chips_.

water

salad

chicken

pasta

chips

3 I've got _salad_. **4** I've got _pasta_. **5** I've got _chips_

18 **Look and write.**

1 What has he got?

pizza

2 What has she got?

fruit

19 **Write I've got, He's got or She's got.**

1 What have you got?

_____

milk.

2 What has he got?

_____

pizza.

3 What has she got?

_____

juice.

20 **Colour. Then match and read.**

1 I've got

a fruit.

2 Mum's got

b cake.

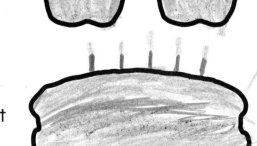

3 Dad's got

c ice cream.

Fun and Games

3:25

1 **Listen and number.**

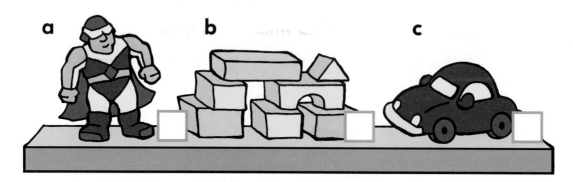

a   b   c

d   e   f

2 **Look at 1 and write.**

> action figure   ball   blocks   car   puppet   train

1 This is my ___car___.

2 This is my ___ball___.

3 These are my ___blocks___.

4 This is my ___puppet___.

5 This is my ___actionfigure___

6 This is my ___train___.

3 **Listen and circle. Then sing.**

What's In Your Toy Box?

Kim, what's in your toy box?
Have you got a plane / bike?
No, but this is my blue car / game.
And where's my grey train?

Kim, what's on your toy shelf?
Have you got a ball / doll?
Yes, yes, here it is.
And here's my purple doll / car.

Kim, what's on your table?
Have you got big blocks / stuffed animals?
Yes, and these are my puppets / trains.
My favourite's Mr Fox!

These are my favourite toys,
Purple, green and grey.
I share my toys with my friends
And I play every day!

4 **Draw toys.**

Story

5 **Read and write.**

1 Where's the doll?

_____

2 Where are the action figures?

_____

Look. Circle three differences.

I'm playing with my friends!

I'm playing with my dolls!

6 Read and number.

a

1 It's under the desk.

b

2 They're on the shelf.

c

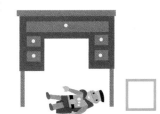

3 It's in the toy box.

7 Write in, on or under.

1 _____ **2** _____ **3** _____

4 _____ **5** _____ **6** _____

8 Circle the words and write.

1 x x x i n x x x x x x x   _____

2 x x x x x u n d e r x x   _____

3 x x i n x x x x o n x x   _____ _____

9 **Trace and draw.**

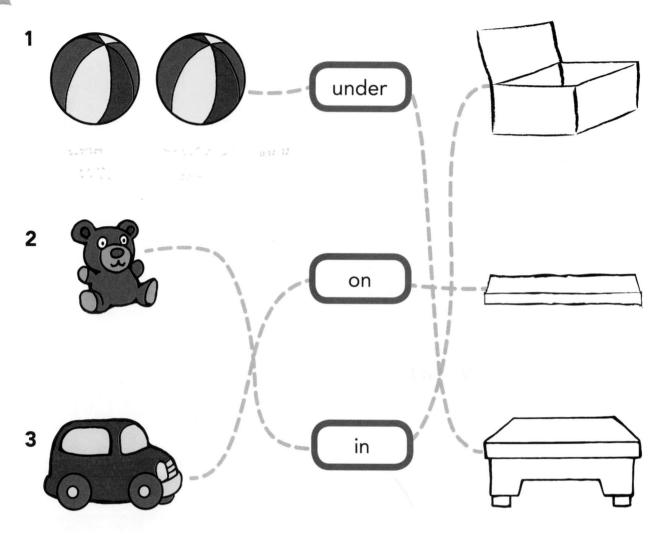

10 **Look at 9 and circle.**

1 Where are the balls?
The balls are **in / on / under** the table.

2 Where is the stuffed animal?
The stuffed animal is **in / on / under** the toy box.

3 Where is the car?
The car is **in / on / under** the shelf.

11 **Read and match. Then colour.**

a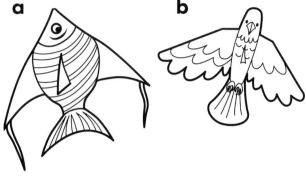
b
c
d

1 This kite looks like a butterfly. It's purple.

2 This kite looks like a bird. It's yellow.

3 This kite looks like a dragon. It's red.

4 This kite looks like a fish. It's blue.

Guess. Then join the dots and write.

THINK
BIG

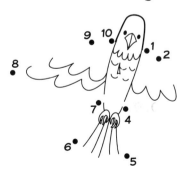

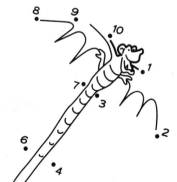

1 This kite looks like a _____.

2 This kite looks like a _____.

12 **Match.**

a

b

c

1 OK. Thank you!

2 Sharing is fun!

3 Here's my car. Let's share.

13 **Draw.**

I share my toys with _____.

14 **Find and circle the letters qu, x and y.**

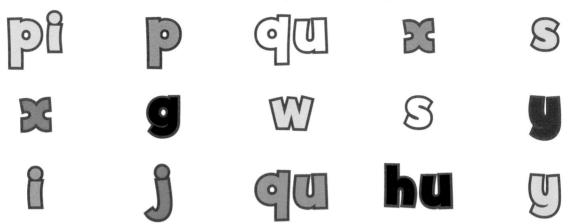

15 **Read and circle the letters qu, x and y.**

1 six **2** quick **3** yell **4** box

16 **Match the words with the same sounds.**

1 quick   **a** yes
2 fox   **b** box
3 yum   **c** quack

3:42
17 **Listen and chant.**

Six quick foxes,
In a yellow box!

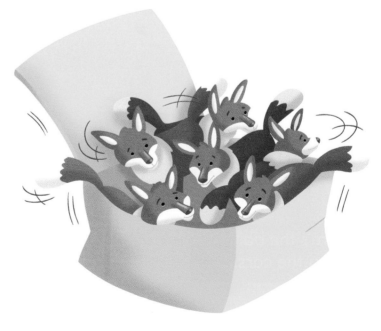

18 **Look and match. Then read.**

John's toys

1

2

3

4

5

a action figure

b ball

c blocks

d plane

e bike

Jane's toys

6

7

8

9

10

f stuffed animal

g train

h doll

i puppet

j game

19 **Draw.**

Where are the cars?
They're in the toy box.

Where's the ball?
It's on the cars.

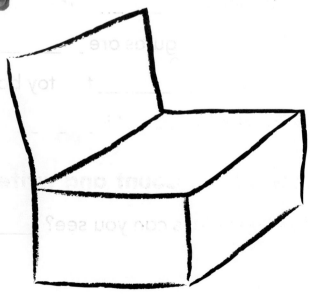

Listen and number.

3:44

21 **Look at 20. Write in, on or under.**

1 The plane is _____ the shelf.

2 The action figures are _____ the chair.

3 The ball is _____ the toy box.

4 The stuffed animal is _____ the chair.

22 **Look at 20. Count and write.**

How many toys can you see? _____

unit 9 Play Time

1 Follow the path. Write.

catching   dancing   hitting   kicking   riding
running   singing   skating   skipping   throwing

1 catching

2 throwing

3 hitting

7 Skating

6 singing

5 dancing

4 kicking

10 running

8 riding

9 skipping

2 Listen and sing. Then match.

Play Time Is Cool!

We like play time at our school.
Skipping and dancing,
Throwing and catching.
Play time is cool at our school!

I'm throwing the ball.
It's so much fun!
Are you hitting and running?
Yes, and it's fun.

We're kicking the ball
And trying to score.
It's so much fun.
Let's play some more.

Chorus

1
2
3
4

3 Look at 2 and write.

1 She is _____ the ball.

2 He is _____ the ball.

3 He is _____.

4 She is _____ the ball.

4 What are you doing? Draw and write.

I'm _____

_____

5 **Read. Then write.**

I'm Not Tired!

1

2

1 What's Patrick doing in picture 1?

He's _____.

2 What are the boys doing in picture 2?

They're _____.

3 What are the boys doing in picture 3?

They're _____.

What do you do before bed?

THINK BIG

Look at me.
I'm _____.

6 **Look and ✓.**

Is Tom skating?

☐ Yes, he is.
☐ No, he isn't.

Is Jen skipping?

☐ Yes, she is.
☐ No, she isn't.

7 **Look and write the answer.**

Yes, they are.
No, they aren't.

1

Are they playing?

_____

2

Are they jumping?

_____

3:55

8 Look, listen and circle.

1

Yes, he is. /
No, he isn't.

2

Yes, she is. /
No, she isn't.

3

Yes, they are. /
No, they aren't.

4

Yes, they are. /
No, they aren't.

9 Look and write.

1

Are they playing?
Yes, _____.

2

Are they kicking a ball?
No, _____.
They're skipping.

10 **Find and write the words. Then do the actions.**

1 b l m i c

Let's _____.

2 p i s k

Let's _____.

3 e d h a n d s e k e i

Let's play

_____.

4 o h p h c s c t o

Let's play

_____.

5 g t a

Let's play

_____.

THINK BIG

Draw and write.

Let's _____.

11 **Match and write.**

drink   enough   food   sleep

1

a Get enough _____ and _____.

2

b Get _____ exercise.

3

c Get enough _____.

12 **Draw.**

I look after my body.

13 **Find and circle the letters ss, z and zz.**

14 **Read and circle the letters ss, z and zz.**

1 fizz **2** mess **3** zap **4** miss

15 **Match the words with the same sounds.**

1 zip   **a** zap
2 buzz   **b** hiss
3 miss   **c** fizz

 3:65 **16** **Listen and chant.**

Buzz goes the bee.
Zip, zap!
It misses me!

17 Look, read and number.

1 He's catching a ball.   **2** He's throwing a ball.

3 She's kicking a ball.   **4** He's skipping.

5 He's singing.   **6** She's dancing.

18 Draw an activity. Then write.

I'm _____.

3:68

19 **Listen and number.**

20 **Read and ✓ or ✗ for you.**

1 I get enough exercise.

2 I play hide and seek.

3 I play hopscotch.

4 I get enough sleep.

5 I get enough food and drink.

6 I play tag.

THINK BIG

1 Look, find and number. 🔍

2 Look and ✓.
What has he got?

My Party List

☐ cars
☐ a bike
☐ a game
☐ a puppet
☐ a train

🔍 **TOYS**

1 action figure

2 bike

3 game

4 puppet

3 Think and draw.
What is in the present?

PARTY FOOD

5	cake
6	fruit
7	juice

PLAY TIME

8	catching
9	kicking
10	throwing

What **is** it?   It**'s** a chair.

1 Write and colour.

1 What is it?      ___ a marker pen. It's blue.

2 What _____ it?      ___ a ruler. It's yellow.

3 _____ is it?      ___ a backpack. It's red.

4 What is _____ ?      ___ a crayon. It's green.

5 _____ _____ it?      ___ a pencil. It's blue.

6 What _____ _____ ?      ___ a book. It's red.

2 Join numbers 1 to 10. Look and circle.

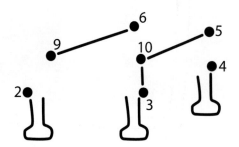

What is it?

It's a **chair** / **desk**.

> **How many** brothers and sisters **have** you **got**?
>
> **I've got** one brother.
> **I've got** two sisters.

1 **Write and match.**

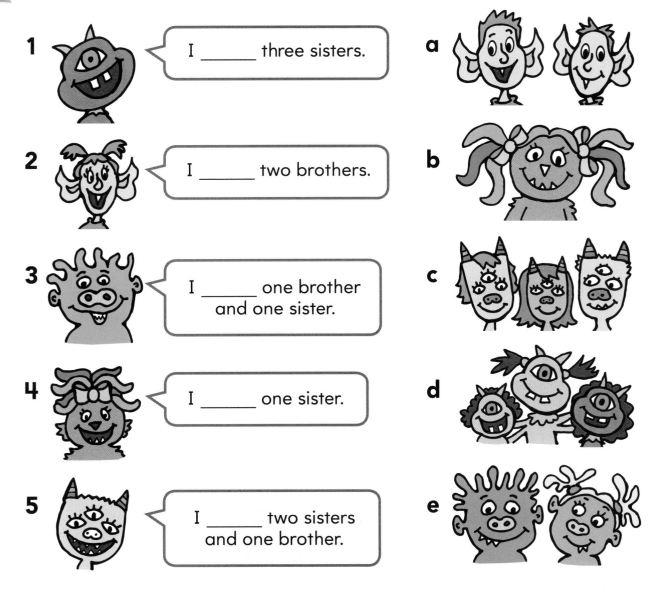

1 I _____ three sisters.

a

2 I _____ two brothers.

b

3 I _____ one brother and one sister.

c

4 I _____ one sister.

d

5 I _____ two sisters and one brother.

e

2 **Draw a monster family.**

3 **Look at 2. Count and write.**

How many monsters? _____

Has she **got** long hair?	Yes, she **has**.
Has he **got** short hair?	No, he **hasn't**.
Has it **got** a small head?	Yes, it **has**.
Has it **got** a big head?	No, it **hasn't**.

1 Look and match.

1 Has she got a long nose?

2 Has she got short hair?

3 Has she got long arms?

4 Has she got big feet?

5 Has he got a long nose?

6 Has he got short hair?

7 Has he got long arms?

8 Has he got big feet?

Yes, she has.

No, she hasn't.

Yes, he has.

No, he hasn't.

2 Look at the dog. Write.

1 It's got long _____.

2 It's got a big _____.

What **are** you **wearing**?   I**'m wearing** a green hat.

What**'s** he/she **wearing**?   He**'s**/She**'s wearing** white trousers.

1 **What's she wearing? Write and colour.**

1 _____ a red blouse.

2 _____ a yellow skirt.

3 _____ brown shoes.

2 **Read and colour.**

What are you wearing?

I'm wearing a red jacket and brown trousers.

I'm wearing an orange dress and purple shoes.

What **are** you **doing**?	**I'm** reading.
What**'s** she **doing**?	**She's** making lunch.

1 **Look and write.**

1 What are you doing, Jim?

_____ water.

2 What are you doing, Ellen?

_____ a book.

3 What are you doing, Ben?

_____ my teeth.

4 What are you doing, Pam?

_____ to my dad.

2 **Look at 1. Write.**

1 What's Jim doing? He's _____.

2 What's Ellen doing? _____ reading.

3 What's Ben _____? _____

4 What's Dad _____? _____ watching TV.

What**'s** the duck **doing**?	It**'s swimming**.
What **are** the cows **doing**?	They**'re eating**.
What**'s** he/she **doing**?	He**'s**/She**'s running**.

1 **Look and match. What are they doing?**

1

a sleeping

2

b running

3

c swimming

4

d eating

2 **Read. Circle and write.**

1 What's he doing?   **He's / They're** _____.

2 What are the cats doing?    **She's / They're** _____.

3 What's she doing?   **She's / He's** _____.

4 What's it doing?   **It's / They're** _____.

What **has** he **got?**	He**'s got** milk.
What **have** you **got?**	I**'ve got** juice.

1 **Look and write.**

1 What has he got?   He's got **cake / milk**.

2 What has she got?   She's got **fruit / pasta**.

3 What have you got?   I've got **pizza / chocolate**.

4 What have they got?   They've got **crisps / juice**.

2 **Write 's got or 've got. Then match.**

1 I _____ juice.   a

2 She _____ chicken.   b

3 They _____ chips.   c

4 He _____ ice cream.   d

Where's the ball?	It's **in** the toy box. It's **on** the shelf. It's **under** the table.
Where are the cars?	They're **under** the desk. They're **on** the sofa.

1 **Write Where's or Where are. Then match.**

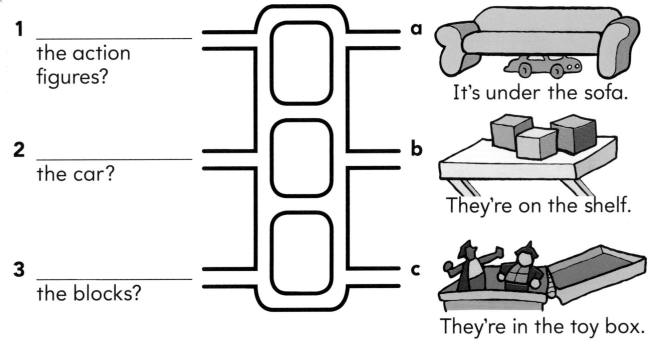

1 _____ the action figures?

2 _____ the car?

3 _____ the blocks?

a It's under the sofa.

b They're on the shelf.

c They're in the toy box.

2 **Look and write in, on or under.**

1 Where's the ball?

It's _____ the desk.

2 Where are the balls?

They're _____ the desk.

3 Where's the ball?

It's _____ the desk.

Is she **singing**?	Yes, she **is**.	No, she **isn't**.
Are they **dancing**?	Yes, they **are**.	No, they **aren't**.

1 **Read. Look and write.**

1  Is she throwing the ball?

Yes, she

_____.

2  Is he running?

No, he

_____.

3  Are they sleeping?

No, they

_____.

4  Are they skipping?

Yes, they

_____.

2 **Look at 1. Write Is or Are. Then answer.**

1 _____ she eating?

_____

2 _____ he reading?

_____

3 _____ they climbing?

_____

4 _____ they running?

_____

My BIG ENGLISH World

1

My name: _____

My age: _____

ME →

ENGLISH
AROUND ME

Paste or draw things with English words.

CINEMA TICKET

1 Good Morning, Class!

2 My Family

3 My Body

4 My Favourite Clothes

My Favourite Unit:

My Favourite Words:

• hello • goodbye • pencil

• stuffed animal

• skipping • finger

long • mum • pizza

FOLD

5 Busy at Home

6 On the Farm

7 Party Time

8 Fun and Games

9 Play Time

My Favourite Project:

How are you?

What's your favourite colour?